My *Mending* Broken Pieces

My Journey to Wholeness

TRINA SAN

Published by Victorious You Press™

Printed in the United States of America

ISBN: _ 978-1-952756-33-7

For details email vyp.joantrandall@gmail.com

or visit us at www.victoriousyoupress.com

Contents

Acknowledgements

This book would not have been possible if it were not for God, who put the vision in me years ago to tell my story to help another woman. Next, I want to thank my wonderful husband, who always believed in me, loved me unconditionally, and pushed me on days when I wanted to sit still. Lastly, I also want to thank my children and grandchildren for being my cheerleaders; even when things weren't going well, they were always there for me. I love you.

Dedication

Dedicated to every woman who ever thought or believed they were less than anyone or who didn't feel as pretty as the next woman. God does not look at your outside. God looks at who you are on the inside—how you treat others. God already knows who you are supposed to be. God wants you to realize your potential and what you can accomplish as long as you put Christ at the center of your life. You are beautiful and amazing; just trust the process!

Introduction

This is not one of those books you will want to curl up with in your favorite chair and blanket. You know, the blanket or quilt—the one you have had for years that nice and soft, yet worn out in several places. It is like the shoes you bought some time ago, and now that you have broken them in, it is time to buy another pair. You won't need it because this book will challenge you in ways that you may not have been challenged in a while. It might even make you mad. You might even need some tissues. However, while you are looking within — those dark places in your mind and spirit that you overlooked or say you are doing fine — no issues or concerns, and your life is great; it may not be. So I will challenge you to look anyway because sometimes we can fool ourselves into thinking life is great when, in fact, there is one thing that you wanted to keep a secret.

Like many people, I know what went on in our house, and life stayed there, and you were not to speak about it to anyone outside of the house. So, to the outside, the family was the best, but to the ones who lived in the house, they knew differently. That cycle continued until I was grown and raising my own family.

When I was living with my first husband, I went through many challenges in my life, and at times, I wanted to quit. You will read how I made it through those difficult times. God was with me even when I didn't acknowledge it. My knees should have been bloody because of the many times I cried out to God to stop the pain. I wanted my life to be easy, but it wasn't for many years. There was infidelity, lies, alcohol, and a lot of eating mixed with fear, doubt, and insecurity. I asked God many times why I had to go through a divorce or why didn't He fix him and make him come back?

As you walk through my journey with me, those events brought a lot of emotional, physical, and spiritual disconnect, but healing occurred as God put my broken pieces back together. Some missing pieces needed to be replaced, and you will read how God did that as well.

I hope my story will encourage you if you are going through some troublesome times or have been through some challenges. I pray that you believe there is more for you than what you are experiencing today!

Chapter 1

THE SET UP

"DAD, NO—STOP!" I cried out. *Wait! What just happened?* I thought. *I'm afraid!* It happened just that fast. One-minute dad and I were sitting at the kitchen table - I was about eight or nine at the time—the next minute, dad was holding a knife to mom's throat as she was serving him some vegetables to go with his steak. She was lying on our orange, brown, and yellow linoleum kitchen floor. As I sat at the table in amazement and fear, I could also see the look of fear in mom's eyes.

At that age, I couldn't have articulated what emotions I felt, nor what mom was probably feeling at the time, nor did I know how it affected me. The events preceding dad's outrage are unclear. Perhaps mom got into dad's liquor stash in the attic or basement, or maybe she said something to him that set him off. I know that my seemingly simple happy life as a child changed the rest of my life. That traumatic event shaped me and my future relationships, school performance, self-esteem, and ambition for years to come. One thing is certain; I remember it as if it had just happened yesterday. I don't know what came over dad that evening, nor do I know what or if mom said anything. This was one of those moments that was never spoken about beyond that day. I learned to keep secrets from that day forward.

Secrets kept for year after year can grow into a humongous monster that can eat you alive until you self-destruct—quietly. This is a terrible place to spend over 30 years of your life. While I was unaware of it, God was with me that day, and God has been with me every day after since. My secrets were also lies. I lied about where I had been and who I had been with unless I felt it was acceptable.

Mom had lost her mom at a young age, and she had to take care of her father as a young girl. Her aunt and uncle raised her the remaining years of her life and were important to mom, especially since her dad had died at a young age. She had lost most of her family prior to my birth, and the only family she had remaining was a nephew. Mom and dad were married in their 20's, and they began raising a family immediately. They had six children but raised five as one of their children died as an infant. It's possible that traumatic event affected her for the rest of her life.

My mom was diagnosed with a mental disorder when I was 12 years of age. As the voices became more prominent, she drank to calm the voices in her head. When mom would hear the voices, she would shout aloud, which caused me a lot of anxiety. I was the last one at home, and I didn't have anyone whom I could go to and discuss these situations. Often, I would call my sisters in a panic to come and help mom. When mom had these outbursts, dad was not home as he was either working for a party or at an Alcohol Anonymus (AA) meeting. Where were my older sisters when I needed them? I wanted someone to save me from the chaos going on internally and externally. Fear, doubt, and insecurity robbed me of peace at a young age.

Although mom had her challenges, she always kept a clean house and prepared dinner every day except Friday or Saturday, when she would prepare a hamburger or hot dog for the two of us.

There were many nights a friend of mom would come to visit with a fifth of liquor. This also caused me a lot of anxiety, and I hated to see her coming. She would drink so much; her husband would have to come over to take his wife home.

I have heard, over the years, that FEAR is an acronym for False Evidence Appearing Real. I have to say, there was nothing false about that knife at mom's throat that night, and there was nothing false about mom screaming at the top of her lungs at the voices while I tried to study or watch television.

Although Dad and I went to church every Sunday, we did not talk about God in my home. Dad was a deacon at the Baptist church, and mom was raised in a Methodist church and often spoke of foot washings. The expectation was that I would attend Sunday school and church every week unless I was sick. There were times when I did not want to attend church, so I said that I was ill. At the time, I found church boring, nor did I have any friends in my class. I felt out of place around the other kids because I didn't know what they knew about the Bible. That's how I felt in school, too—constantly feeling alone in a crowd. How does a child get through life when they have to deal with so many unsettling events at home? Who do you talk to about those feelings? While there may be more services available today than it was in the '70s for children, some may be afraid of any repercussions from asking for help.

At some point, I realized that if I had my nieces or nephews over to spend the night, mom would stay sober, and dad would buy treats. I wanted to be daddy's little girl, but my sister before me had already occupied that place in daddy's heart.

The events I experienced as a child are classic for a counselor who would have seen me for at least five sessions. This also set me up so the enemy could manipulate me into believing the lies that I am worthless, ugly, unloved, dumb, boring, shy, and fat for many years, but Jesus! God reminded me of who I am through Jesus Christ and not because of something someone said or did. I am a victor, not a victim. I have been chosen—chosen by the Most High to share my journey that has taken my broken pieces and put them together to find freedom!

Chapter 2

THE BEGINNING

I was born in the year 1964 to an average middle-class black family. My mom was 41 when she got pregnant with me, and my dad was 42. It was nothing exciting or extraordinary about my home. Although they had bought a house so that our family did not have to live with my grandmother. My parents loved my four siblings and me, although I was the "baby" of my parent's children. It wasn't until I was an adult that I thought I was not supposed to be here because my sister closest to me—11 years older—used to tell me I was a mistake. Instead of looking at my birth as a mistake, I see where I was more of a blessing to my mom and dad. You see, before I was born, my mom and dad had been separated, and my mom was post menopause—so she thought. They got together for a night of passion, and here I am. My birth not only brought my parents back together, but I had a beautiful daughter at 18 that brought my mom a lot of happiness, especially when she was dying from lung cancer.

When I began school, they bussed me miles from home, as this was the beginning of segregation. I remember our buses being the last to go into the school and sitting in the back of the classroom. In my first grade class, my chair was near the bathroom, and a little white boy stuck his penis out of the door to show it to me. I am not sure why he did it, but as a six-year-old, I was not interested or curious. I played with boys often since I had several nephews. I also had some nieces, but I connected more with boys growing up because they did not judge me.

An ordinary day after school was like most other children, except mom worked for a few years prior to being diagnosed with a mental disorder. When she wasn't home, I went to a neighbor's house until someone came home.

If I didn't complete homework before my parents arrived home, I did homework until dinner or until I completed it. I rode my bicycle, went to the park, roller skated, and played games with a friend—nothing extraordinary with the naked eye.

In elementary school, I was a chubby girl, and my neighbors and friends of my parents reminded me of that often when they

would comment about my chubby cheeks. My mom shopped for me in Sears and Roebuck in the "pretty plus" department as other stores did not carry clothes to fix my awkward body. There was nothing pretty about those clothes. Here was another reason for me to feel insecure about who I was; again, the enemy had been working on me for years. There was no one in my life who said, "Trina, you are beautiful." I did not hear those words until I was an adult and the wrong people told me, and I discovered they only wanted one thing from me. Since I did not love myself, I thought giving myself to them was what I was supposed to do. I was so confused and misguided.

Elementary school often brought other issues for me. I was taller than my other classmates. I was heavier than them as well, so I always felt different. The only time I felt like I belonged was when I played ball with my nephews and the boys in the neighborhood. The guys never looked at me as being "fat" or "ugly"—they accepted me the way I was. Often I wondered why I wasn't thin like the other girls. When I was in elementary school, the teacher would weigh you in front of the other classmates, and everyone would know how much you weigh. While I don't know how much my weight was, I do know that I was larger than all the other girls in my class.

Mom and dad did not comment on my size or what I ate until I reached junior high school. In junior high school, mom noticed I would eat watermelon down to the rind, and she

mentioned that it was not good for me to do that and I could have more. At that moment, a switch turned on that said, "I need to hide how I eat." I began eating with my head in the fridge so no one could see me. Please note it was dad, mom, and I who lived together, and dad wasn't home during the day. More fear, doubt, and insecurity manifested in my mind; yet, I didn't gain much weight during these years—although I thought I had.

There were times when I would get out of bed to get some gingersnaps or little sandwiches for a late-night snack. I ate in my bed under the covers while my parents were asleep in the next room. The reliance on the food to get through the feelings was just one way that I coped. Many days I could be found on the sofa watching television, biting my fingernails, and sucking my thumb.

The older I got, the more the fear and insecurity plagued me. In junior high school, boys used to touch my body between classes within a crowd, so I could not see who it was. I felt uncomfortable eating in the cafeteria, so I stay outside when weather permitted. The one thing I had going for me during those days was I could run—fast. The fear kept me from trying out for the track team, but I would show my skill during gym class—people thought I was great. I attempted to "fit in" but never did. Boys would tease me on the school bus, and I would want to fight them.

During those days, I was in the academically gifted classes, which required me to be above average. The fear, doubt, and insecurity were magnified even more. Unfortunately for me, the teachers knew my family. There were not many places I could go without someone knowing my family name. I interpreted that as "you are special because you are so and so's niece." This carried me throughout my life, yet it was not as painful as when I was an adolescent.

In high school, my grades suffered because life got more challenging for me. Although I lost weight during the summer, I still felt like I did not fit in with the other students, nor did I know how to be an individual. I did not go to parties, sports functions, or clubs. The best times for me were in JROTC. The sergeant and lieutenant treated everyone the same, and I found my place within these students. It was helpful that my best friend was in the same class. I excelled in this class, and I thought I would join the Army when I graduated; however, I feared leaving home.

When I was a senior, I was the only senior in my JROTC class, and the sergeant put me in charge of the class. This was the greatest thing that ever happened to me! Here I am, the leader. I made sure my uniform was always the best and taught the cadets everything I had learned as a sophomore and junior. High school is a time when girls want to go to their prom and look forward

to the senior events leading up to graduation—this was not my path. I did not go to my prom, but I did attend the military ball.

I only dated two guys in high school, and only one of them attended my school. However, I was the talk among the boys in my sophomore year because a senior told everyone what he did with me in my bedroom. I lied about it because I was so embarrassed. The boy did not want to be my boyfriend but to use me. I avoided his house like the plague since we lived in the same neighborhood. I began to hate myself more because my efforts to try to fit in did not work. What was it going to take for me to love myself?

Chapter 3

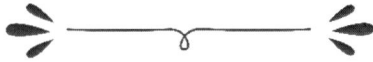

We lived in a middle-class black neighborhood where everyone looked out for you and any other children in the community. Most of the adults there knew each other well and would be quick to discipline you. We kids ran in the streets, jumped rope, rode our bikes, played football, baseball, and made mud pies growing up. I also spent time with my nephews and other boys and did what they did. I caught butterflies, fireflies, and frogs. It sounds like a normal childhood. It was average to most people, but inside the four walls, it was different for me. As a matter of fact, this is a life many young children had, and you were fortunate if both parents still lived in the home. I loved my childhood, especially when I had someone to play with.

Mom stood about 5 feet 5 inches tall and was a wonderful, loving, kind, and gentle homemaker who had been diagnosed

with acute paranoid schizophrenia when I was approximately 12 years of age. My mom was a very modest and quiet woman who was an excellent cook and housemaker. She wanted to make sure I had a good childhood, so she took me on the bus to the amusement park, movies, shopping, and downtown to just have a hot dog and fries at Woolworths. Mom worked as a housekeeper for a family for many years until it was no longer possible for her to work because of her disability. When I was out of school for teacher's workday or holiday, I would accompany her to her employer's house to work with her. My work involved playing with the dogs—two Great Danes.

Dad stood about 5 feet 7 inches tall, who resembled Martin Luther King, Jr., in my eyes, only lighter skin. He was a recovering alcoholic and catered parties for the upper echelon, and quite often, he was paid to purchase the liquor before the event. There were times he would bring the remaining bottles home to use at another party. He drove a nice car, worked every day, had a bank account, was a faithful, tithing member of a religious organization, was friendly to everyone, and even had a sense of humor. He worked for many years to repair the damage of his past mistakes. He had a round belly and always smiled. He also did a lot of community service, which made me want to do those things when I grew up. Maybe you had a home like this— it looked good from the outside, but there were skeletons in many closets.

My home was not always the happy, loving, peaceful, and model home that others would want their life to look like if they knew what was on the inside. However, for most of my life, I remembered all the good times, and there were really good times.

The most memorable times were during the holidays. Our home was filled with laughter, and our house was exciting! We managed to have approximately 20 people, including my sisters and their families, in my parent's two-bedroom, one-bath home for many years to enjoy laughter, games, and meals. Occasionally, my dad's brothers would come by to just pay their respects. How we managed to fit everyone in the house and no one complained about it is a miracle. I guess that was a testament to the love in there. Mom would begin preparing for the holiday meal the day before, and you could smell the various aromas that would make you salivate in anticipation of the end result. She would prepare the cornbread that was going to be used to make the dressing and chop any vegetables that she was going to need the morning of the holiday. I believe she got up at 3:00 a.m. to make sure the turkey, dressing, rice, gravy, sweet potato pies, and collard greens were ready at mealtime. The last time mom prepared a holiday meal was two years before the Lord called her home. During that time, I was given the opportunity to prepare a couple of the family's favorite dishes for them to enjoy. It was a blessing to be able to learn from mom and receive any guidance

to make sure it was just like she would have prepared them. While the memories of these times remain with me, the dishes have been passed on to my daughter.

During mealtime, the children would sit at a card table in mom and dad's small bedroom with four chairs for about seven or eight children. Yes, I said four chairs! The adults sat in the kitchen in addition to eating on card tables seated in the den. There would be a football game on for all the sports fan playing. Once dinner was done, there was always a spade game going on at the kitchen table. We children would hear the adults in the kitchen because dad was always accused of cheating, but no one would challenge him. These discussions would always lead us to join them for a short period to see what the commotion was. It's amazing what one can do with so little, but no one would have ever known we didn't have a three-bedroom house with two and a half bathrooms. Life was great as long as I had family around. I still love family time. While I loved family time, I felt insecure, fearful, and lonely when I did not have them around.

My sisters sensed I needed things to keep me busy, so they bought me crafts and a sewing machine for birthdays and holidays. To this day, I enjoy creating things. I have crocheted, written poetry, painted, did macrame, needlepoint, and anything else I could do to keep me busy. Some of that busyness led to some unfavorable and destructive activity.

That loneliness eventually led me to a place of doing things that compromised any beliefs my parents had or what they desired for me as their youngest child. I believed what every boy said. If he made fun of me for being a virgin, I showed that I was not. If he said he loved me, I believed him. If he said, "If you love me, you will have sex with me." After I did this time and time again, I lost a piece of me every time. I didn't know how to say "no" and stick with my convictions. I did this to myself until I was an adult. Men, boys, lies, fear led my life into darkness over the years. Maybe you can identify to a degree. The enemy thought he had me, but God had another plan.

At the age of 17, I told my mom that I wanted to have a child to feel loved. She responded by telling me I was crazy—mom had given birth to six children and raised five. I went to Sunday school and Bible Study, but nothing changed. I accepted Christ in my life when I was 16, but I was so insecure and shy that I didn't even tell my sister, whom I was visiting for the summer.

The following year, I got pregnant with my daughter. When I married at 22, I wanted to get out of my parents' home. You are probably thinking, why didn't I get my own place—my mom was against it. I went from being taken care of to trying to figure it out. This is from a woman who did not even know who she was or how to take care of anyone but her child.

During my first trimester, my mom suggested that I have an abortion; I didn't want to hear what she had to say. I did, however, prayed about it for a night or two when something miraculous happened. While watching television one afternoon, a commercial came on that was on pro-life, which I was not aware of at the time. The commercial was what I later found to be the story of the unborn child. A day or so later, a gentleman came to our door carrying a Bible. My dad had answered the door and asked this Caucasian, tall, and broad gentleman to come and have a seat in the living room. The living room was the place where only guests were allowed to sit. A little while later, dad called me from my bedroom to join them. I don't remember much of what he said, but he did hand us a printed copy of the same story I saw on TV. Oh, my goodness! This was the answer to my prayers. I knew later that day that God had sent this man and the commercial to tell me that I was not to abort this child. My mom was not happy with my decision, and I had not told my dad yet. Not only was mom not happy with my decision, but she also did not talk to me for about ten weeks—until it was no longer possible for an abortion to take place.

Since I am a natural people-pleaser, I did not want to disappoint my dad, but he did something I didn't expect-we went shopping for furniture. I didn't feel like I deserved it since I was a "bad" girl, so before dad paid for the furniture, I told him, and he let me know that he already knew. Well, wouldn't you know mom had already informed dad, and he still bought me the furniture. The only thing my dad ever wanted was for me to be honest with him, and most of my life, I had difficulty with that. I lied because I was afraid. The one statement he made that hurt me to my core was, "I had always told people that you were a good girl, and I spoke very highly of you—now I can't say that anymore." Boy, was I disappointed by his words. Tears ran down my cheeks, and I thought about that the rest of the day. Mom and dad were wonderful during my entire pregnancy.

I had been dating a nice guy, who was a virgin, while I was pregnant, and he even asked me to marry him. All was going well, so I thought until he met another woman and moved on. That was one of the many times I felt abandoned and less than. When my child was born, I continued to live with my parents, although they wanted to send me to live with my sister and her family in another state to attend college. They even discussed adopting my child. Thank God her husband said that it would cause too many issues and decided against it. My parents did more for me and my daughter than I ever expected while we lived there. They paid for all our expenses, and my dad even told me that I should not work for a year to experience the important events of my daughter's life. Before my daughter, I did not honor my parents like the Bible states; but later, I realized how important it was to do so. I wanted my days to be long. I did everything I could to make my parent's life easier.

While I was going to community college, I met a man. He was ten years older than I, and he was married. I didn't know initially that he was married, but it flattered me he wanted me. I met him while driving to work. He waved at me. Because I was insecure, it was great whenever I got any attention because it meant someone thinks that I am beautiful. The enemy doesn't rest and knows precisely how to set you up right. I didn't stop the first time nor the second time, but that third time I pulled my car over off the highway to talk to him, a stranger, and gave him my phone number.

I felt like I had just won the lottery. It was great when he called me that evening. My parents would have forbidden me from talking to him if they knew how much older he was. He said all the right things and came to see me at school during my breaks, and we would sit and talk and sing—it was so romantic. Shortly after meeting him, I asked if I could call him, and he said it wouldn't be a good idea. He had told me he and his wife were separating, but not yet. I fell for it until I didn't like it anymore. I got up enough nerve a few months later to tell him I couldn't see him anymore. It would not be the last time I would see him.

Chapter 4

Life to others looked great but, I continued to deal with more internal issues than most. This life set me up for future relationships that would not end well. When a boy tries to rape you, and you fight to get away, they would call that Post-traumatic stress disorder today. Those stressors of not being able to express feelings kept me in bondage for many years. One relationship after another, but rarely short-term—same guy, different name and face. Does that sound familiar to you?

There is the charming, smooth-talking, and gentle one who could talk your panties off. Then there is the rough yet loving man who took control yet treats you like a lady, only to find out later that he did that with other women as well. Let's not forget the intelligent, witty, and slick gentleman. He is the craftiest of them all. He might say, "I love a woman with whom I can have meaningful conversations. That's a turn-on for me." Oh, brother!

I believe I am an intelligent and beautiful woman today, but that was not always the case. While I grew up in a home where you were to attend church services every week, I did not have a relationship with God until I was much older. When one has a relationship with the Lord, other relationships can be healthy. Those former relationships were meaningless and a way to hide my genuine feelings of fear, doubt, insecurity, disgust, anger, and lack—the need to compare my insides to someone else's insides constantly.

I got tired of compromising myself and feeling low that I took some time off from dating—various times. I wanted to be a better person, a better mom, and I wasn't sure how to do that because mom did not know how to talk to me about relationships and forget talking about sex—mom was "old school." How does a young woman change the feelings inside and act differently without direction or mentorship? Not only did I not know how to have healthy relationships with men, but I also did not know how to forge friendships.

A single stay-at-home mom, living with her parents and carrying several deep dark secrets from her past - shaped her as a young woman. During this period, my dad heard about a program through the United Way that taught individuals skills to use as a word processor. The word processor was new, and they needed skilled people to fulfill the new opportunities. This program allowed me to secure a position with a top organization where I was employed for several years. A broken woman who looked like she had it all together. Everything is going great since I am working for a Fortune 500 company, driving a car, attending church, have a couple of friends, and a beautiful daughter.

A FEW MONTHS LATER, after I started working there, a coworker told me that she had some single brothers. "Girl, you have a brother? Why had you kept that secret for all of these months?" I exclaimed to my coworker. You see, I had been single since my last breakup because I was tired of the losers I had met. She agreed to give me his number and him mine—that was the beginning of a long-term relationship that would end up in heartache.

I was a little upset with her because she had kept them to herself. I did, however, end up meeting one of her brothers, whom I married six months later. I know now that I wasn't ready for anyone, but God will give you the desires of your heart if you ask. I also know that it is extremely important to write and make plain the type of person you desire in your life—character, spiritual beliefs, children, etc. My only requirement was that he loves my daughter as much as he loved me, had a job, and went to church. Write the vision and make it plain. My vision was very vague, and I got what I got. He wasn't a bad person but may not have been the right one for me.

Chapter 5

He was 5 feet, 11 inches tall, handsome, a red-haired, freckled-faced man with a gap in his teeth. I knew the day we laid eyes on each other that I wanted to be with him. We were married six months later. We didn't have much money, but we were willing to make it work no matter what because we loved each other. My mom used to say, "Girl, love, don't pay no bills." I thought she was being harsh, but she was telling the truth, I later found out.

Marriage, I thought, was the answer to all my internal problems. I have the key to make all that is wrong on the inside right. I believed that everything that was lacking within would be fulfilled in this marriage. That was so far from the truth. As a matter of fact, the marriage made those issues worst. The Bible says that we should "seek the kingdom of God first and all His righteousness and all other things will be added to you." (Matthew 6:33) The Bible does not say accept a man's hand of marriage, and you will have a perfect life. It also does not say seek things first, and God will come next. This scripture is not only crucial for relationships but any and everything. It was also the belief that if I just go to church weekly, Bible study, sing in the choir, and volunteer in other organizations, all will be well.

Our relationship probably started like others, not much money, but loved one another so much that the money did not matter. We had to work and budget and do without nice things sometimes. My parents continued to help us by taking my daughter shopping when she was with them. Some days when I didn't want to be alone, I would hang out at their home and enjoy mom's home cooking. One would probably call me spoiled. Well, maybe I was because I would go to my mom and dad to ask for money without my husband knowing it. After all, I never had to do without anything when I was at home. Don't get me wrong; my husband was a great provider. He worked his regular job and would tend bar for private parties and a catering company. He did whatever it took to make sure the family always had food on the table. Our prime rib may have looked like liver and onions. Both of us worked hard and played hard when we had a little extra. He was a hard-working man like my dad. One would say that I married my dad in more ways than one. My dad was a provider but not much of an affectionate person, just like my husband. They weren't affectionate towards their wives, at least, but with other women, they were. Not only was he like my dad as a provider, but I found out later that my dad liked other women as well.

Most weekends, my parents did me a favor by keeping my daughter, so I could get adjusted to being a wife. The only issue was, my husband went out most weekends—drinking, and I was home alone. As I stated previously, I was already insecure, so that did not help at all. Since I was a homebody, I didn't go to clubs regularly—I enjoyed being at home and taking care of my family. Consequently, his idea of fun and my idea did not line up, so we usually did separate things on Friday evenings. I now know it is important to have some like interests in a relationship. It is also essential to discover what fills your spouse's love tank and, just as important, what fills your love tank.

We didn't have a lot of money since he was new to the city, and I had just secured a position—the lack of money and being alone just fed my insecurity and fear. I remember thinking to myself one day: *If this is what marriage is like, I want out.* I wanted to leave him, but I was too afraid to say anything. Not to mention, I was in love with him. I believe I was more in love with the fact that he loved my daughter as much as he loved me. Remember, I didn't know who I was, so I can be anyone I need to be for anyone no matter what the cost.

As I look back over my life and my family, I think many of us had the same mindset that if he paid the bills, took me out to dinner, took care of the yard, or bought the groceries, it was enough. I have learned that good is the enemy of best, and I deserve the best God wants for me. I no longer have to settle for "good enough." God can and always will provide the best for me—for you! The Word says that God provides food for the birds and a nest to lay their heads, so does He not care for us more? If that is true, I believe it is, then God will give me the desires of my heart, and He does not lie, nor does His Word return to Him void.

When I've had conversations with one of my sisters, we discuss a time when all our husbands were having a discussion outside, sharing their dirty secrets. During these conversations, many of the guys admitted to having an affair, including my former spouse. When a person is guilty, they only disclose what the others said, not his dirt. When people say, "Love is blind," they were talking about me. I did not believe my husband would have an affair, and I trusted him.

After being married for six months, we got pregnant with our son. It was a joyous time for us to complete our family. Most of the years following were pretty uneventful. We rented a house and then purchased our first home after our son was two years old and our daughter was seven. Periodically, we would have friends and family and play old school music, but we also loved family time. We knew our neighbors next door, across the street, and a few houses down the road. Their children would often come to our house for snacks and drinks, especially in the summer. I was the mom who tried to direct a few children who did not have manners or who needed speech therapy. One of my friends down the street would watch my son, and I would watch her daughter.

However, it was in this home where I experienced my first incident when I questioned my husband's fidelity. One evening while waiting for him to come home from a party, I received a phone call from a woman asking for him by name. This evening, I had planned for us to have a picnic in the living room since the children were asleep. He came in the house shortly after the telephone call—these were the days when we had to have a landline. When asked about this woman, his first question was, "Who did they ask for?" *What did that matter?* They asked for him by his first name, which he did not use. His response was they had the wrong number. I could not argue with that since his name had been confused with another man a few times.

I was doing things to keep our marriage fresh, which is vital to keep from getting bored in your marriage. I bought sexy lingerie, stayed up late to greet him, continued to cook, clean, and keep myself up. It surprised me when he advised me he did not want to be married anymore. My response was to ask who it was that he was spending his time with now.

35

Sometime later, he came home one day and told me that I needed to get a shot. I asked what kind of shot, and he stated for venereal disease. I told him I didn't have a venereal disease that I was aware of, and he proceeded to tell me that he did. What's funny about this whole exchange is that he said that it was probably from me. When did I have time to do anything with anyone else? I worked a full-time job outside of the home and then a full-time job when I stepped into the house. I went to get the shot at our doctor's office and didn't question anymore—at least not out loud. I believe from this moment on; I did not trust him. However, I stayed married many years after that incident.

Prior to purchasing our second home, my dad told me that he was cheating on me, and I didn't believe him either. Of course, I found out later that he had been cheating on me. There was even a time when he told the children and me that he was going away for a few days, and he didn't know when or if he would be back. He stated that he did not want to be called because he needed some time to think things over. The children and I cried. I was full of questions with no answers. I did attempt to call his mobile phone, but he either had it turned off, or he just sent me to voice mail. He was gone for three days. He returned as if nothing had happened. He answered no questions, and we did not speak about this time afterward. This is very painful to write because I realize now how low my self-esteem was. Thank God I am not in that same place.

A couple of years later, I was surprised by two things. He pulled out new/different underwear that was nothing he would have typically worn. He indicated that a friend of his recommended them to keep things alive in the bedroom. The next thing he said to me the same day was that he wanted to wear a condom. *What? Why do we need a condom?* At this time, I should have questioned more, but I just kept my eyes and ears open, so I thought. The charm and love blinded me. Love was blind for me. If it had been a snake, it would have bitten me several times, and I might have still missed it. This is where having my mom or talking to my sisters would have been helpful.

A year or so later, I began to feel uncomfortable and had sores on my rectum and surrounding my vagina. I was diagnosed with a debilitating venereal disease. How could this have happened? I had not been with anyone else other than my husband. When I went to the doctor, she examined me and prescribed medication. The nurse who was left in the room with me told me that my husband was cheating on me if I had not been with anyone else. I want to say that I was angry at him and believed what she said, but I did not. Don't judge me. I wanted to believe that my husband and the love of my life was not having sex with other women. I was in shock! When he got home, I informed him what the doctor and the nurse said. Of course, he denied it adamantly. He even called the nurse a name and said she needed to mind her own business. It's obvious I was very naïve. *Why would my husband cheat on me? My wonderful man is not so wonderful after all.*

After finding out he had been having an affair, we were grocery shopping, and a woman stared at him as we passed in the aisle. I looked at him and asked him who she was. He, of course, denied knowing who she was. I turned and asked her what was she looking at? He said to me to be quiet because I didn't know her. It's amazing what you cannot see when you are blinded by love and deceit. How could this be happening? We had a lovely home and wonderful friendships. We lived in a quiet neighborhood. I sang in the choir, and so did he. I was suffering silently. I gained a lot of weight over the years because of fear, doubt, and insecurity.

I wanted to leave him, but I didn't know how I was going to make it. He made a lot more money than I did, and I was comfortable, but I was uncomfortable while being comfortable. So, what did I do? I said, let's go to the beach for our anniversary. His response was only to ask how we were going to pay for it? We always went away for our anniversary, and it had not been an issue before now. We were celebrating 14 years of marriage. We made the reservations and finalized the trip. This was one of the worst, if not the worst, trip he and I had. They gave the hotel room I reserved to another couple because we were late getting there. He was never late, and it was probably because he had to take care of his mistress before we left. We found another room, which he paid for, and we slept in separate beds. I have never felt so alone in a hotel room with another person. I could have gone on that trip alone and had a better time. When we had sex, it was as if he was having sex with a stranger that he hated. Even the pictures we took looked like I was miserable. I eventually gave those pictures to my son because they were very painful memories for me. He could not have loved me, although we made the best of the trip.

Often, it is easier for me to avoid an issue than deal with it directly. This only hurts me. The other person goes along as if nothing has happened. As long as I take a back seat and keep quiet, nothing changes. A week later, another bomb was dropped on me. The day following his birthday, I came home to find my home in a bit of disarray, as my children often did. When I entered our family room to the right of the foyer, I noticed everyone's favorite green chair cushion turned up on its side. When I went to put it back down in the chair, I saw an envelope with my husband's name on it. I opened the envelope and read the card—my heart stopped. I sat down on the side of the chair as my hands shook and read it again and again.

I wanted to call him at that time, but I decided to wait until he got home. Since it was Monday night, I knew that he would be home a little late because he had a Masonic meeting that evening. It was around 8:00 p.m., and I decided to call anyway.

"Hey. Who is L.R?" The response on the receiving end said, "What are you talking about?" I said, "You must know who it is because she gave you a card," and I proceeded to read it to remind him. He was home in about 10 minutes on a typical 20-minute drive. Oh, how someone can remember something when their feet are to the fire.

The anger and rage that was displayed caused me a lot of anxiety. I can't say that I was ready to experience his wrath and lies. I wished that I could say this was the only time he was unfaithful, but it was not. I want to say that I had enough confidence to give him an ultimatum, but that did not happen either. I stayed, and I forgave him. Both instances would have been enough to end the relationship, but I stayed because I didn't think I could manage without him. The trust I had earlier in the marriage had been nonexistent at this point. He said I would have to forget and not bring it up again. I wanted to know why. *Why was I not good enough? What was wrong with me?*

Oh, he abided by my requests for a while, but then he got anxious and needed to go out with his friends. I told him to go because he was unhappy staying home with the kids and me. How many know that you can't keep a wild animal caged? Where was God in all my turmoil? Why is He letting this stuff happen to me? If my mom had been living during this period, I would have had someone to talk to about it. I didn't know how to navigate around it, nor what to say or do. My security did not lie with him but with the Lord. I know that now, but I had no clue what to do, so I continued like the good little wife filled with insecurity and self-loathing. I didn't make any waves, nor did I ask any more questions than I needed to ask.

That same year, my family sold my dad's home, and we divided the proceeds equally. I wanted to surprise my husband for our fifteenth anniversary with a cruise.

Things had gotten better, and we were working on our marriage. I would venture to say things were going well. He had not been staying out late. I had found no money in his pockets, and there was some peace in the home again. But no sooner than I thought things were getting better, it switched again to the same old inappropriate behavior. Here I was, a wife and mom of two children, and I couldn't show up for them when they needed me.

My older daughter needed me to help her navigate her issues, but I was too consumed with trying to make my husband want to stay home with us. He had started going out to bars and coming home late. My intuitiveness told me he was not faithful again, but I wanted to believe otherwise. What's next?

Chapter 6

"Am I not pretty enough?" I asked God. Maybe I'm too fat—that's it. I will lose weight, and then he will want me back. I don't know why I wasn't good enough or just enough. I know that I did not make him go outside of our marriage; yet, he did. Perhaps I became too busy with volunteering at church and my children's school. Maybe I didn't make him or the family a priority. Not only did volunteering at church take a priority, but so did volunteering at school. I became a human doing and not a human being. When was I supposed to have time to spend with my husband, my children, or my friends? There was no seeking God first. However, whenever there was a women's retreat, I was there too because that was the answer. I could never understand how all the women who attended appeared to have the relationship with God that I so wanted. There was one women's retreat that changed and transformed me that I will never forget. I think we must be so broken and out of solutions to reach total surrender for God to change our hearts and minds so that He is all we can see. Nothing in God's world happens by mistake.

If you are separated, going through a divorce, divorced, contemplating it, or if your marriage is on the horizon, this is for you. In the 23rd Psalm, David says, "He leads me beside the still waters and restores my soul," which is precisely what God does. Perhaps you have not had that experience yet. What I would say is to take at least fifteen minutes every day, twice a day, and seek God's face—especially early in the morning before the sun gets up and your day gets too busy.

Pray, ask God to speak to you, and listen—really listen. Quite often, we want to give God a laundry list of things that we want and need.

This is not the time to do that.

God already knows what you need before you ask Him. I am not saying He does not want to hear your voice because He does. God loves to hear from His children, and He cares for your every need. God said, "Come unto me who labor and heavy laden and I will give you rest. Take my yoke upon you and learn of me for I am meek and lowly in heart: and you shall find rest unto your souls" (Matthew 11:28-29). You may not believe that you are worthy of the knight in shining armor, or the peaceful life, or the house on the lake, or the fine car, or just to have friends that truly love you, but you do deserve that and more. God would not withhold any good thing from His children. God created you and me to be used to build up His Kingdom. Whether your significant other hits you, yelled at you or called you out of your name, that doesn't change who you are to Jesus.

Marriage is like baking a cake—every ingredient is essential. There must be love, kindness, patience, long-suffering, honesty, trust, and most of all, communication. If you leave something out, then the cake will not turn out as good as it would if they were all added. All parts come together to make a whole. There is not one ingredient more important than the other as there is not one person less important either. If we are apart from Christ, we fall.

After 16.5 years in the same relationship, I wanted to know what happened and what I could have done differently, but I did not get the answers I wanted in the timeframe that I wanted. The marriage was a facade for me and anyone else who looked at us every Sunday at church. However, I was the one who was being fooled, or at least not true to myself. We were both miserable with a smile on our faces after our first ten years of marriage. Let me be clear—I was in love with him. He was my all in all. God should have been my all in all. I wanted it to work. I wanted to be married to my friend. The pain that is felt during a separation and divorce is unmeasurable and is the same as when someone dies. The process is the same—denial, anger, bargaining, depression, and acceptance, but you can still see them either on social media or in person.

I did not go through this process one time. I went through these cycles many times. I did not reach acceptance until I went through several cycles and decided it was time to move on. There was a part of me that was missing when the end was upon us.

If you never really cared about your significant other, you will go through the grief process a lot quicker and easier. It takes time to go through or guidance on how to handle the hurt, pain, disappointment, blaming others and yourself—whatever, whomever.

This is a time to take an inventory of your good characteristics and your not-so-good characteristics. Seek God daily for guidance. I don't want anyone to get tripped up because of any religious prejudices you may have or concerns because you already have a religious body. This is not about religion but spirituality. It took me some time to realize that God wants me to commune with Him regularly. You may ask what that means or how to go about it. For me, it was reading the Bible and sitting quietly first thing in the morning. God wants to guide my day and wants me to know that above all, God loves me more than anyone else. As I stated earlier, it took me quite a while to realize that I was trying to do what I wanted to do and not asking God for guidance. I wanted my life to look like I thought it should look. I am an adult woman; surely, I can figure out what is good for me. I was totally misguided. The enemy wants me to think that I could.

Remember when Jesus was out in the wilderness for 40 days, and Satan tried to tempt Jesus to do his will and not respond as the Word of God. However, Jesus reminded Satan of the Word as well. I brought this out because there were times that Satan told me it was okay to talk on the phone to a married man or a man in a committed relationship. I fell for it for a short period, and then God would remind me of who I was through a message. I would then feel convicted by what I was doing. This is what happens when you are not studying the word and grounded in spiritual principles.

There were things I did that I would not have done before—doing drive-bys at his apartment, gained access to his email and sent messages to his "friend," and said some "choice words" that I would not have said. During this time, I started to gain weight and overeat due to my depression and self-loathing.

One day I was sitting at home "eating" and feeling sorry for myself when I heard the Holy Spirit asked me, "What are you doing? He's over there enjoying himself, and here you are feeling sorry for yourself." *Wow,* I thought. *You are right. I need to get it together!* It was then I started to walk and change the way I was eating. I felt empowered about what I was doing and ready to move forward with my life or at least accept what was in front of me.

There were several occasions that the Holy Spirit was informing me of what was going on, and I was so wrapped up in believing him that I would not listen. I was in such denial. Denial is one of the stages of grief that can keep you stuck in one place. When you are hurt, you want everyone else to hurt because it is forbidden that someone else would be happy and enjoy life.

Why couldn't everything go back to the way it was. I would ask. I wanted my family back together. It did not take long for me to hear the Holy Spirit remind me of the pain I was in within the relationship.

Before the separation, I took a trip to the beach for four days to seek God's direction and get some answers. When someone drops a bomb on you that will change your world, it's time to take some time for yourself—no television or anyone else around. The worst thing you can do is seek guidance from others because they haven't gone through your journey or experienced your pain.

There were times I wanted him to hurt as much as I was hurting. The difference between me and the others where I showed my emotions loudly. I wasn't going to go without you knowing how much I was hurting. The trip gave me a little more courage and strength through God. It wasn't until this trip; I realized that I could make it without my husband. I didn't know how difficult it would be financially or emotionally, but I knew that Jesus was my savior, and with Christ, I can do all things.

The separation would have gone a lot easier if he had not stayed at the house for another two months—those months were torture. Every day I woke up, and he was still there, ironing his clothes and getting dressed for work. I wanted to move gracefully during this time, but I didn't, nor could I. I cried. I yelled. I stalked him and his mistress after he moved and lied about it many times. I hated who I had become.

Here I was, 41 years old and alone. Alone with my thoughts and myself!

After being married for 18 years, including the year and half of separation, I became a more confident woman after deciding to move on and stop the unhealthy behaviors. Although I was married, I did exhibit some loneliness within the relationship. It was not until later when I realized that I did not know who I was. I had been a mother and wife, but I did not have an identity of my own.

The children introduced me as their mom (no name). The spouse introduced me as the wife, again, no name. I even started introducing myself as I am so and so's mom or so and so's wife.

What had become of ME?! *Who am I?* I did not take care of myself—not like I do today. I took baths and got my hair done, but I did not take special care of myself to make sure that I spent quality time with my "daddy." God told me who I was in His word. He said, "I am a chosen people, a royal people, a holy nation God's special possession…" (1 Peter 2:9a). Does that not sound great?! The first time I heard that was at a women's retreat. However, it took years of falling, living a facade, and gaining 80 pounds for me to really hear it

Chapter 7

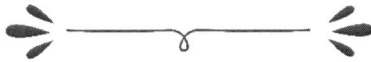

BROKEN RELATIONSHIPS

The first relationship that was broken was that with Christ. I left the relationship before I was married. God would often give me nudges to let me know that He wanted me to join Him in the morning, but I was too tired or too busy to stop.

Other past relationships left me empty, alone, depressed, and despondent. What I realized throughout the process of the relationships I had encountered is that those individuals were not good for me nor did most of them deserve me. My issue was I did not realize how much being in a relationship with them was keeping me from the destiny God had for me. This revelation did not occur right away, and quite often I would forget with each relationship. I would say the words "rejection is God's protection." While I believed those words, my actions did not demonstrate my faith that God would bring the right person or persons into my life. I cannot have mountaintop experiences staying in the valley of despair, fear, anger, resentment, self-loathing, or insecurity.

My security is not tied to any person or job or financial standing. The Bible states the battle does not belong to either one of us but the Lord. Who can fight a battle better than I can? My Lord sees and hears all. He knows when I am hurting and how I am feeling. Believe me, whatever situation is occurring, God already knows it, and He is not surprised about the situation. Quite often, I set the pattern of this vicious cycle because of my insecurity. I had conversations with men that were less than holy and sanctified. When that took place, they saw me as a sexual object, not as a lady nor someone who respected themselves. I don't want to paint a picture of me being a loose woman, but I was a woman who did not set boundaries. I said one thing and did another. I would often say, "I am not going to have sex until I am married. "I meant it when I said it, but when I was in his presence, and we were alone in his home or mine, a kiss would lead to the next thing. I would hate myself afterward and would repent for what I had done. Perhaps you can identify with doing the same thing.

The best way to avoid being in situations that would compromise your belief is to never be in a location alone with the other person. If you are out in a public place, you will be less likely to be tempted.

We must realize that God loves us no matter what we look like, how we feel, or what we think. However, God wants us to know for ourselves is that we know who we are and whose we are. Ladies, we were bought with a price—a hefty price—Jesus! I challenge you to look in the mirror and stare at yourself for five to ten minutes and tell yourself what God says you are.

YOU ARE BEAUTIFUL (PSALM 45:11)

YOU ARE ENOUGH (2 Corinthians 12:9-10)

YOU ARE LOVED (Jeremiah 31:3)

YOU ARE WONDERFUL (Psalm 139:13-16)

YOU ARE SPECIAL (Ephesians 2:10)

Don't get me wrong—I accepted Christ in my life when I was 16 years old while visiting my family up north. I got pregnant later because I did not tell anyone that I had accepted Christ in my life; therefore, I did not receive the biblical teaching I needed once I returned home. I constantly needed and wanted love and attention from my spouse, and he could not feel a God-sized hole no matter how much he did. He bought me jewelry, and that was not enough. He paid all the bills, and that was not enough. It was so terrible that my fear, doubt, and insecurity pushed him away. I did not know how to have a crucial conversation with him about anything that may have been controversial. It is in the tough times that you grow. What do you do when your significant other comes to you late in the evening and says that he does not want to be married anymore? What is the first emotion? My first emotion was anger! I was furious because I knew it was another woman. Since I did not know who I was, nor did I believe it if anyone told me, I cried every day. I had lost my best friend. This was the person who told me who I was and showed me how to be that person. If you have ever been in that place or are there now, STOP. Stop believing the lie that you are less than. I do not want to give the enemy any more credit than he deserves, but he is the author of lies. He is the only one that will tell you that you are not good enough or aren't pretty enough, or whatever the lie is that is playing in your head. Now is the time to really seek God for answers and directions. Please remember, God never leaves us nor forsakes us, but I could not see the forest for the trees and was blinded by the tears, the hurt, and the anger.

Watch out for the pitfalls that tell you to find out what is going on, even if you think you know. Only God can give you the answers you are seeking. Be prepared because God will show you if you ask and are willing to hear. I have to warn you—this process can be pretty painful. What do you do when you are in your feelings, and your "so-called friends" are not there to hold your hand or wipe your tears or tell you, "Girl, it is going to be okay." When you are all alone, wipe your tears and pull yourself out of the fog because you did the best you could, and you only have God to lean on. I know it does not sound reassuring to some but to others it will bring comfort; however, for me I wanted answers. I wanted to know: *Why me?* I wanted to know how this could have happened. I cooked most days, I had sex regularly with my husband, we laughed and cried together, we went to church together. I would say, "God I want answers!" I remember being stopped in the middle of my tyrant only to hear, "Why not you? "I stood in silence for a while and repeated those words out loud, "Yeah, why not me?" God chose me for a better purpose. I did not know for what purpose, but I knew that my pain would turn around at some point. I just wanted the pain to end now.

Amazingly, I went on with my life and would be doing fine, and then the enemy would send that person back in my life to disrupt my peace. The cycle began time and time again of mending and being broken again. This cycle continued until I decided I did not want to play in his playground anymore.

Ladies, you have a choice. You do not have to entertain an individual, male or female, that does not honor or respect you or your decisions. I delayed my healing by continuing to allow him in my space. During those times, I would feel good for the moment but then reality would remind me that he is going to his apartment while you continue to hold things down at the house. I wanted the pain to end. The pain was not going to end until I went through the process. You see, there is no easy way to get to the other side. If the easy way is taken, there is not any growth or refining. When gold is refined, it is done by fire or through a chemical method. God took a quiet, obedient, meek, insecure, and depressed woman into a strong, confident, humble, loving, kind, and focused woman.

For many years I was going through the refining process. I have been burned more than I can count. I get back up again. After I have a fall, I rise again and notice that I have changed a little more. I was not a pushover like previously, but I still had some imperfections that kept me from growing. I was still looking for approval from others, or I wanted to be liked by everyone.

I went through years without even one friend. I had friends before my divorce, and then there were none. It's funny how that happens. He was still visiting the friends because he was invited, but I was no longer invited after a birthday or two. It was a lonely place. As I said, God will remove some things and some people away so that the only one you can lean on is God. I must admit I was very resentful at those ladies, but I have come to understand or at least have compassion for them. It is quite possible that they felt awkward inviting both of us, so they chose him.

There were a lot of financial roadblocks for me during this period. The salary that I brought in was not sufficient to maintain the home where my son and I resided. I am grateful that he paid the mortgage until the house sold a year later. I really started to feel free from that relationship after I moved into an apartment. Now was my time to "show him." The only one that got knocked down was me. Prior to me moving into an apartment, I bought a car—a car that I could not afford, but I needed. I was seeing a man who lived one state away but had never been married. The truth is this man never wanted to give up his freedom because if he had, he would have already been married. He told me that he had not found the right one yet. By the way, he had a teenage daughter, so he had been with someone at some point. His only issue is commitment. I have this innate ability to find the most unavailable men alive. I seem to have this other ability to attract the married, separated, drug-addicted, and lying men out there as well. These relationships have all been a part of my refining and maturing into the woman God wanted to use to build up his Kingdom. It was my job to study God's Word and practice it in my relationships, job, career, home, and in church. God took a little seed, watered her, fertilized her, pruned her, and she became this beautiful flower.

I used to go to women's retreats year after year, looking for the answer to the question that stayed in my mind day after day. I wanted to know how these ladies have such a close relationship with God. They all seemed to have it together, and I wanted to have what they had. I would study the Bible with friends at lunchtime and pray with them weekly, but nothing changed. This was not the first time he had a relationship outside of our marriage. I have spoken to many women who decided to no longer have another relationship after their partner committed infidelity. The enemy wanted to keep me bound in fear, doubt, insecurity, and stuck. I have to admit I was in a whirlwind of one bad relationship after another because I was still broken and confused. The only one that creates confusion is Satan. God does not give us the spirit of fear or confusion. If these emotions are present, it's time to reevaluate your relationship.

Chapter 8

Crazy is as crazy does. After years of being single, my cycle of fear, doubt, and security continued. I met a man with whom I later became engaged. He was a very kind, honest, trustworthy, loving, and hard-working man. I became restless and discontented with the relationship about one year into our relationship. During this restless period, I entertained conversations with another man. We later began spending time together but did not have sexual relations. I excused my behavior time and time again, but I felt guilty.

One Sunday after church, I went to visit this man, and I was in a position that I wanted to say no at first, but then I let him touch me. Soon after I said "No," he did not stop. I left that house angry with him and myself for allowing it to happen. Before you ask did I report it as rape—I did not. That experience reminded me of one I had when I was 15, and a neighborhood boy attempted to rape me. By the grace of God, I had a lot of fight in me, and then my nephews showed up and rang the doorbell. This was a secret for over six years. Those secrets kept me in fear and insecurity. I was afraid to walk past his house for several years. No one needs to live in fear like that. God did not give me the spirit of fear but of power, love, and a sound mind. Unfortunately, I did not remember that when I visited that man's house. You would think that I would not have had anything else to do with him, but he apologized, I listened, and then entertained him again. This just shows how much insecurity I still exhibited after more than five years after my divorce. I had the physical together as I had lost about 100 pounds by this time. I thought I had the spiritual together, but I was missing the Word and my self-worth. I often did not believe I was worth having the man in my life who could love me for me and accept who I was, and not what I could do for him.

I met a couple of guys who were current or former drug addicts—those are really tricky. They are tricky because addicts who are not in recovery will lie and believe the lie, they just told to get what they want from you. If they are in recovery, they deal with fear as well. Therefore, they will probably lie just because of the fear of you not wanting to be with them.

While hanging out with a friend one beautiful, sunny Saturday afternoon, we walk into a used bookstore just to kill some time. When we walked in, she spotted him first—a tall, dark-skinned, attractive, smooth talking man. He approached me and began talking to me and I advised him that I wasn't interested, but my friend was. He stated that he wasn't interested in her. I felt bad for a bit, but gave him my number anyway.

This smooth-talking man spoke to me at the park on our first date and lied to me as if he were telling a short story and I fell for it hook, line, and sinker. I got caught up in wanting to get married that I didn't even listen to the Holy Spirit guiding me to leave this one alone. I asked, "Are you married or dating someone seriously? "He replied he did not. I also asked him if he had a drug problem. I asked because he was missing some teeth, and I've known people who were addicts who had some missing teeth because of the drugs they were using. Well, wouldn't you know it? He said he used to, and his son was currently using. I didn't believe him but continued to see him anyway. The enemy loves a desperate woman. That desperation blinded me and allowed me to compromise my beliefs and the gentle voice telling me to ask more questions and walk away from him if he did not tell the truth.

When I date men, I advise them the one thing that I hate the most is lying. You see, I was a constant liar before I got into the

Trina San

program that I was working on. They advised me to go to God daily for guidance. God would give me gentle nudges to go in a particular direction, and at times, I would do what I wanted to do.

When I go my way, I end up delaying the promises God has for me. I'm sure I delayed them ten years the way I took my will back. The enemy also loves to give you what you want. I wanted a man who went to church and was a believer—I got just that. The only problem was the truth was later revealed. He was separated, not divorced. He lived in a halfway house because he had only been clean for three months. When I received the call from the wife, she told me the truth about their relationship, and she also said he had been seeing another woman in another state. By the time I received her call, I had already ended the relationship because he lied about the halfway house. I would say that I hate that I got involved with him, but nothing that I have gone through has been a waste. I learned a lot from each guy that I dated. I learned what questions to ask and to watch closely. When I am close to God, I know when it's time to move or when to stay. On the other hand, when I am in fear, doubt, worry, anxious, desperate, or lonely, I don't hear from God and make mistakes that lead me back to darkness.

The man who feels so insecure that he has to talk a lot to elevate himself. Our first date lasted four hours, and he spoke about himself and his family most of the time. I don't think I was able to get a word in edgewise. This was the first indication that I should have said, "It was nice meeting you, but I am not interested in seeing you again. "OH, but no, I saw this man several months. It was fun—we played cards, went walking, out to dinner once or twice, talked for hours, and worked out. He cared about his body so much that whenever he came to my apartment, he had his own meat and potato or rice in a cooler in his car. That was the strangest thing I had encountered with a man. There were so many red flags with this one, but I was, again, desperate. I didn't care about his muscles, although my friends thought they were wonderful. He didn't believe in Jesus—red flag for me or it should have been. I began compromising my beliefs even more. We met when I had been a bit confused by things that went on in the church that I decided not to go for a while. This one never spoke about having a job, and I was aware that he didn't have a lot of people that he was training. When asked how he made his money, I was told not to worry about it. That was not the answer I wanted to hear, so I did end the relationship. He got extremely upset with me and sent me these long email messages to tell me who I was and wasn't. I subjected myself to this man one more time, although I knew going in that nothing had changed, and I would get the same thing I did previously. Please don't follow my example. Two statements come to mind when I think of some of the situations I encountered. One is when someone shows you who they are, believe them. The other one is, doing the same thing over and over and expecting different results is insane. For me to change my personality, I needed God to work in me and through me. If I could have changed on my own, I would not have dated some of the men I dated. Sometimes, it's a slow process—I was the slow cooker learner.

Many times, when waiting for the right one to come along, we are either anxiously waiting to say, "When is God going to send my husband," or "Why do I keep meeting the wrong one?" Or asking yourself if he is the right one. Patience and faith are essential during the waiting period. We can also be waiting impatiently. We could be looking at every handsome man or financially sound man as if he were the right man, only to find out he was a sheep in wolf's clothing. He might be abusive or have anger issues. Those issues may not present themselves until after 90 days of dating and winning you over.

After going through several relationships, I have learned that God wants the best for you and me. God will not serve you prime rib on dirty garbage can lid; the prime rib will be on fine China sitting on a crisp, white linen tablecloth. If you are ready emotionally and spiritually and Mr. Right is as well, then God will put the two of you in the right place at the right time. Being ready will look more like you enjoying your family, friends, job, church, and life—content. At the same time, God already knows your heart and wants to feel your desire. Be present for yourself and for those who love you most. Please do not neglect or despise the little things. Don't regret the challenges and mistakes that you may have encountered—they make you better if you allow them.

Love is truly a gift from God, but we need to check with God before we get too far into a relationship—better yet check, with God before the first date. What looks and sounds good may not be good after all.

In my opinion, relationships should never be taken lightly. I have heard people say, if it doesn't work then I will just get a divorce. That is not what God intended marriage to be. Most women cannot handle a "casual" relationship without expecting more from the man. While sex is a wonderful part of a loving relationship, it should not be taken lightly or done outside of marriage. In my experience, most women will not adjust to just having sexual relations with a guy and it being okay with her— there is no commitment. If you say you are alright with it, I advise you to search within to see whether you are being completely honest with yourself. I have been there, and it was good for a short period, but then came the time when I wanted more of him, and that was not possible. What happens when it's Valentine's Day, Thanksgiving, or Christmas and you want to see him? Who do you think he's going to spend his time with? Furthermore, you cannot even tell your family about him without lying about where he is and who he is because someone might know him.

There was a feeling of sadness that came over me when I looked around and my friends were either married or in a committed relationship that they could talk about. What was I going to say? "I'm seeing a man, but he is with his family today?" I could not and would not speak about the nights in quiet spots to steal a kiss and hug for only an hour. Ladies, this was a lonely time all because I did not love myself enough to accept "good enough." When I was at home, alone, God comforted me and told me I was worth more and that He loved me. God's love is everlasting. God's Word from the beginning in Genesis to Revelation He reminds us how much He cares for His children.

God took a rib from the man to create woman—you and me. God has numbered every hair on our head. God loves your thin nose, wide nose, wide hips, slim hips, thin lips, or full lips! Take a few minutes and look in the mirror. You may not like the freckles on your face or the cellulite on your hips or your sagging, chicken cutlet breasts. Instead of looking at what is wrong with your face and body, take a look at the woman you are on the inside. I have encountered many people, especially women, who have identified who I am, but I was not in tune with that person. God put something special in you as well; you just need to look beyond the surface to find it. We are beautiful creatures crafted uniquely. Women would have a better life if we stopped trying to bring down the other woman because we are insecure. Appreciate and celebrate your sister whether she is Caucasian,

Black American, Asian, Hispanic, Guianese, or African. When we come together, we can accomplish the miraculous.

When I think of women in the Bible who did miraculous things, I can see how the hand of God was with them no matter how they started. It is not where we start that matters, but how we finish. One of my favorite women in the Bible is Rahab because, despite her unfavorable career as a prostitute, she put her life and her life of her family in danger. She became courageous and bold by helping Joshua and his men to safety. Because of her faith, God saved her entire family and gave her more than she could have ever dreamed. She later married Salmon and gave birth to a son, Boaz, who became a descendant of Jesus. She reminds me of my past when I did not know how to set boundaries and sold myself short. If her life turned around because of one decision, so could yours, and just like it did for me. I got another chance at a new beginning, and so could you. No matter what your past looks like, it is the past. I could not go forward looking backward; otherwise, I will continue to fall.

I ask myself sometimes: *How did I sell myself so short?* I am not an unattractive woman, and I am intelligent. I loved my dad, but I did not grow up with my dad telling me what a smart and beautiful young woman I was becoming. When I was a teenager, my dad told me that I would always look the way I looked no matter how long I stayed in the mirror. I asked him, "What was that?" He said, "Ugly." That one word stayed with me throughout my childhood and adult life. It has been many, many years, and I still hear those words and can see my dad looking into the mirror with me. No matter what someone may say, words hurt. If someone threw a stick or stone at me, the pain is only temporary, but hurtful words stay with you for a very long time. Those words kept me believing I was worthless. I believed that one word kept me from growing into the woman God intended me to be in my earlier years. Has anyone said anything to you that may have kept you questioning who you are or whether you can succeed? I never wanted my daughter to struggle with self-worth.

When my children were young, I told them they could do anything they wanted to do—the sky was the limit. How many know it is easier for your children to follow what you do not say vs what you say? My children saw me struggle in my relationship with their dad and the pain that I endured so much that they either did not want to get married or delayed it for years. There is nothing wrong with waiting for the right person, but sometimes we can overthink things. I wish I had waited until I was ready. I got married when I did because I wanted to move out of my parent's home and my mom did not want me to go until I was married. This is not a good reason to get married. I realized we should have waited longer to get married. I needed to live on my own for a while so that I knew what it was like to take care of bills and be an adult without my parent's help. I had a job and was content with just my daughter and I—life was not perfect, but it was good. Needless to say, he and I needed to spend more time together to get to know one another. He lived in another state, so we only saw each other on the weekend.

I believe marriage is wonderful when both people come into the relationship whole. When I say whole, I mean each individual is aware of who they are and what they want.

There are several signs I missed while married that may help you identify whether this person is the right one before you take a BIG leap into the rest of your life—till death do you part.

*He spends more time with his friends than you.

*Ex-girlfriend still calls his mom's house and his home.

*He's emotionally unavailable.

*He goes out drinking (says alone) every weekend.

*He works late more than three nights a week.

*When you visit his mom's home, he goes out and leaves you alone.

*He comes to bed late and says, "I was asleep on the sofa."

In the movie *Forrest Gump*, he said, "Life is like a box of chocolates...." Well, so is marriage. You never know what you are going to get one day to the next. One day maybe like milk chocolate—sweet, and the next day maybe like dark chocolate—

a little bitter. However, you can get several days like dark chocolate, and you can choose to keep chewing on them or spit them out. Better yet, you can look at what you had before and avoid it all together. I am not saying avoid difficult times; I am simply stating to avoid your response to things you did prior. The best thing to do is deal with them when the situation arises and let God handle them—don't pick them back up repeatedly. When I do the same thing frequently, expecting a different result, that is plain insanity. I have tried to do the same thing time and time again, and I get the same result. It wasn't until I chose to do something different that I got a different result. If I am on a merry-go-round and I get nauseous, I am going to get off. However, if I do it again and again, it is no secret that I am going to repeat the same cycle. When I get tired of getting sick, then I will stop riding.

Chapter 9

Making a decision was always difficult for me so I would ask for everyone's opinion because theirs was better than mine. So, I would ask friends, "Hey girl, what do you think I should do about this guy? He has a good job, he's funny, he thinks I am beautiful, and he loves me?" What's wrong with those statements? Well, it doesn't sound like anything does it? What did I feel? What did I like? Most of my dating life was just like that—as long as he was interested and likes me that was enough. A friend once said, "You should want to be with him just as much as he wants to be with you." Where and when did I get the idea that that was not the case? This was a case of, "I am not good enough." Quite often I was too trusting, and I let many people tell me what was good for me as I had in my adolescence. Why did I believe everyone's opinion was better than mine? Most of the time their life was not any better. After spending some time with God, I finally realized that Heavenly Father's direction was where I should have directed my questions.

There were times, I must admit, that I knew that that man was not good for me and I didn't want God's direction. When I took matters in my own hands, I would end up angry, hurt, and disgusted.

I have dated a couple of men who wanted to show me a better life; yet I like to control what happens and when. Nor did I trust them or believe that anyone would do that for me—I didn't believe I was worthy. Consequently, one of those men pursued me continuously. He knew he wanted to be with me shortly after we met—not me. I wanted to keep my options open because I didn't want anyone to get that close anymore. We had a relationship for several years then he would get frustrated with me because I didn't trust. I would get frustrated with him because he wouldn't act the way that I thought he should. Here was a gentleman who wanted to show me how to take me home and make money. He had been successful in real estate investing in the past. I would not let go because it was my home--I dug my heels in the ground. No one was going to try to change me or take away what God had given to me. Stubborn is the one word I would describe myself during that time period. I have since let go of the fear that he was out to get me. I would have rather ran him away or put up a wall so high and thick he would not be able to get through. Obviously, God had a different plan.

I began going to a counselor for direction and clarity to navigate through this relationship. It had been many years that I had been involved with someone whom I loved enough to continue to date them. My normal routine was to just find a reason to break it off and move on, but he was different. I wanted out but couldn't release him unlike the others. As long as I could convince you that the relationship wasn't working, and I did many times, then I didn't have to work on me which meant I could remain the same. But this man would say God had assigned him to me and I to him. I would exclaim, "No He didn't! Why don't you just find someone else who is willing to do what you want? "It wasn't until I stopped fighting—a few years later, and just released him that I was able to see God had sent my answer to my continuous prayer for the man he wanted me to have, financial freedom, and love.

Although I had been married for many years and dated many men, I have never had anyone love me the way the man in my life does today. The difference in this relationship and the others is I know who I am, and I know who God says that I am. I also noticed that he was clear about how much God loved him and who he was. Not to mention, he was not afraid to say it. Here was someone who knew the Word and showed it in his actions. I have someone in my life who was patient with my inconsistencies and reminded me that God did not want a lukewarm believer. It was uncomfortable to realize that my words did not match my actions.

Chapter 10

Homeless. How did I end up homeless? As stated before, there was always some security. Security in my dad, security in my husband, security in my job, but what about security in Jesus?

After selling our family home after the divorce, my son and I moved into an apartment. There were many wonderful memories, yet some challenging times, especially when I could not pay rent. I had a significant amount of debt after the divorce, and I overextended myself by purchasing a new car. I did not make enough money to support the lifestyle that I was accustomed to while married. I allowed him to get away with not paying alimony or child support because I didn't have the money to secure an attorney. Believe me, I tried, but because he didn't sign the first or the second set of papers, it was going into the following year, and the money was gone. We managed, but barely. My son was in his senior year of high school, and I wanted him to have a great year. Before the year was out, though, I was tired of struggling with my dependence on food. I was introduced to a program and committed to working on my weight. This was the best thing I had ever done for myself. Most of the time, I didn't care about myself; yet, I would take care of everyone else. When I put myself last, I ended up depressed, angry, lonely, frustrated, and fearful. Quite often, my prayers to God were bargains or pleas. "God, I promise, if You do...I will..." or "God, please make me not want to eat that..." Desperate to find an answer, but wanting to do it my way. While I had been struggling with my outward appearance, I was being served with an eviction notice. Fear gripped me, and I didn't know what to do. Anxious, I told someone what was going on, and she suggested I ask my church. I had grown up in this church, and my pride kept me from humbling myself to ask for help. But I did, and we were able to stay there until the lease was up.

This series of events led me to make a decision to move to another state to start my life over. I thought I needed a change. My son went to live with his dad, and off I went to Kentucky with nothing but two suitcases, my dog, and small personal items that I cherished. A new job, boyfriend, and a place to live. The place to live was not what it was supposed to be. When you trust someone else, you may not get what you want. I ended up sleeping on this boyfriend's sister's sofa in her recovery apartment, which I had hoped would have been a short time. The following day after work, I went to look for apartments in the city. Louisville is a beautiful city but very different from my hometown. The park by the water, the mixed culture, and the events made me excited to be there. The apartment I located wouldn't be available for a couple of weeks, but I was ready, ready to start my new life in the Bluegrass state.

After being there for one day, I discovered this man had lied to me about having a job. Words cannot express how angry I was, but I didn't leave because I had a good job. Here I am accepting some foolishness from a grown man. I could have stayed in my city. A week later, I found out he had lied about having a child. When God doesn't ordain something, the pieces begin to fall apart. I couldn't leave now. I was in orientation on the job, and I didn't have anywhere to live if I went back home. This was only the beginning. About two weeks later, he had found a job—finally. OH, but no transportation, so I would pick him up, reluctantly, every day. Many days I just took my time getting there—I didn't care. Resentment and despondency were upon me." God, what am I going to do? "I really thought I heard the Holy Spirit direct me to Kentucky. Maybe the Holy Spirit was guiding me to move from that apartment because someone was out to hurt my son. OH well, I'm here now, and I needed to make the best of it, especially since I enjoyed my job.

If that wasn't enough, one evening, I asked him to go to the store to pick up a small bag of dog food. Disclaimer, before I moved, he had me give him access to deposit money into my bank account. Needless to say, when he went to the store, he used the money in my bank account to pay for the dog food and didn't tell me. Oh, and he had the nerve to get extra! The next day I needed some meat for dinner. While in the store, I heard a small still voice say, "Check your bank account." I knew what was in my account, but I checked anyway, and wouldn't you know it? That joker had taken money that didn't belong to him. Immediately, I called him and gave him a piece of my mind while standing in the meat department. Yet, I continued to talk to him. I probably continued because I was sleeping on his sister's sofa, and I couldn't see how to get out of that until I moved. The next time he betrayed my trust, he took more money out of my bank account after I had given him one of my paychecks to move my belongings from my apartment to Kentucky. This was the last straw. I didn't find out until two days later that he had taken one hundred dollars! This man was really testing my faith and recovery. I knew that it was time to go, but I wanted to do the right thing on my job and give them two weeks' notice. Here I am, a 43-year-old woman with no money to get back home. My daughter had wired me money to get my blood pressure medication and enough to get back home. This experiment was a flop that I did not want to repeat. Here were more broken pieces—doubt and insecurity. This would keep me from trusting another man with any part of my life, nor would I ever want to move again unless I was going alone. That could have been the end of the story and happily ever after; instead, it was the beginning of a wilderness journey I pray no one ever has to experience.

Although these events were like a daytime nightmare, I learned some valuable lessons along the way. The only issue with these lessons is that I kept people at arm's length. If it looked like they were getting too interested, I found something wrong with them, and they could have been the gentlest person in the world. Not only were these events nightmares, but they also fed into my issues with abandonment.

Abandonment is one of those emotional life situations that can keep you bound and stuck if not addressed. It can be recognized by pushing others away, people-pleasing, the lack of trust, insecurity in a romantic relationship, and codependency. The first time I felt lost and abandoned was when I was about four years old. My mom, middle sister, nephew, and I lived together for the first few years of my life. My nephew (who is about six months younger than me) and I were inseparable. When we were growing up, I even played with army men, race cars, picked up frogs; whatever he did, I did. Fondly, I can remember he and his brothers would spend the weekend with us, and we would play games and sit in front of our wall furnace. The furnace sat in the hallway, and periodically it would fire up like someone lighting a gas stove. That sound would prompt us to run and sit down to enjoy the warmth. Three children trying to crowd around a heater less than 3 feet wide—those were the good old days.

In the summer, we played outside until the streetlights came on or until we were tired—quite often, it was after mom flicked the lights for us to come in the house. We spent our days running the neighborhood. We would go to the store if we had some money, play football, softball, or ride our bikes down the street and jump the hill. It sounds dangerous, and it probably was, but it was a slight hump in the field across the street, and we would go to the top of the road and pedal as fast as we could then jump the hump attempting to land on the back wheel. We would see who could do it better than the others. I was a little tomboy until I reached puberty.

Since my siblings were older than I, he was the closest to a brother that I had in my life. Once my dad and mom got back together and bought a house, I was extremely lonely. We used to play together all the time. This separation brought me a lot of sadness. This was probably the beginning of my fear and insecurity. Perhaps you have had experiences in your childhood that shaped you; that may not have been revealed or was kept hidden for many years. As I write this, I cannot help remembering the many nights I was awakened, yelling out for nephew and saying, "Come back." While we are not as close as we were as children, we still are close, like sister and brother.

The second time it happened when my sister got married, and her husband accepted a job after college in another state hundreds of miles away. She had been at home sleeping in the same room with me for ten years. What was I going to do now? Yes, I was happy about having my own room, but I missed my sister. I had been a pest to her because of our age difference, but I liked having her around. My sister called me a mistake for many years, but God had a different plan regardless of what she thought or said at 11 years old. One of the few times I said that, I didn't care, but the tears spoke volumes. Not only was she leaving, but she was taking my nephew, whom I had babysat for many days—abandoned again. Another piece of me broken.

The third time abandonment changed my life was after a boyfriend who had professed his love to me and wanted to marry me began dating another girl while we were still in a relationship. During our relationship, he would always invite his best friend and his girlfriend to double date. I was cool with it most of the time, but one day I asked him why did he always ask them? He didn't have a reason. When he and I first met, his parents did not want him to date me because I was pregnant, and he was a virgin. You don't meet too many men at the age of 18 who are virgins. He was very green, but a very kind and loving gentleman. Once his parents had the opportunity to sit down with my parents and me, they found that I came from a good home and I was a wonderful woman. While there are no accidents, a few months later, their daughter got pregnant out of wedlock. So, this kind gentleman decided he didn't want to be with me anymore and left me for another woman. Hurt, bewildered, sad, and lonely—again.

The fourth time I felt abandoned occurred when my mom died. My mom was my rock. How was I going to go on without her? The months preceding her death, she told me that she was tired. I knew what she meant and told her that she could go nowhere. In the next few days following our conversation, Holy Spirit told me to let my mom go so that she could be free of pain. I fought God over this because I didn't have as many years with my mom as my siblings. I felt robbed. *Why do I have to let her go now? I'm sorry I wasn't always a good daughter.* I loved my mom. After all, Mom took care of me when I was sick. Mom made the best hamburgers in the world! WHO's going to make the sweet potato pies that she prepared every Thanksgiving and Christmas? What about the country ham, grits, eggs, and biscuits made from scratch? WHO's going to cook that for me before church on Sunday? Everything Mom cooked was done with a lot of love. I had so many questions, and I was hurting. After shedding some tears, I let my mom know that it was okay for her to leave and I would be fine. I had to give her permission to move on. When she died, I had peace because she knew that I was going to be okay. Although it has been over 28 years since her death, I still miss her and sometimes say a few words out loud as if I am speaking to my mom. Fortunately, she was able to go home to be with the Lord in my former bedroom. There were many days following that I would go to the house when my dad was gone and just sit in the room and talk to my mom—another broken piece.

The fifth time I felt abandoned occurred in 2003 after recovering from a hysterectomy, and my spouse notified me that he no longer wanted to be married and did not love me. How could he come into our bedroom disturb my sleep to tell me something like that? I was not the least bit amused, and I was tired. I had had a long day at work, cooked dinner, cleaned some of the house, and a load of laundry before laying my head down at 10 p.m. "Who is she? "I asked. He said that it wasn't about anyone else. OH really, I thought. This man must think I am stupid. He had been sneaking phone calls before I got home then hung the phone up abruptly when he realized I was standing at our bedroom door. He started eating out every night and coming home late. One night he even had the audacity to come in with the morning sun. I could have let it go but I deserved more respect than that so I informed him that he would no longer do that in this house. I also let him know if he decides to come in after midnight that I would lock all of the doors including the storm door, which he did not have a key for.

Wouldn't you know he didn't believe me, so I locked him out one night and I acted as if I didn't know how the door got locked? Believe me, he didn't try that anymore. During this time, I continued to pray, but I already knew what was going on; however, it was easier to stick my head in the sand and carry on as if it was all good. That year was a devastating year and a happy year. Shortly after he notified me that he would be moving, my grandson was born. The many broken pieces from this relationship gave me a wake-up call. God took my sadness and turned it into joy—that was over 17 years ago.

After over 40 years of being "stuck," I have finally decided to change. That man does not make me who I am or not—only God defines who I am and who I become. I get to choose which way to go. It is important to identify moments that have kept you from all God has for you. Maybe it wasn't a romantic relationship, but a job. You might have been told that you were in line for a promotion—the chosen one—only to find out they chose another candidate. This has only been identified in the last few years because always masking and hiding behind food. The less I felt the more I ate, the more I ate the less I wanted to feel. One day I had had enough. I was morbidly obese at 234 pounds. I did things I am ashamed to tell others, although I have. Enough was enough. There were too many broken pieces, and it was time to be the person God wanted me to be, but how was I to do that? Lost, abandoned, a nobody.

I stayed on a job for about seven years that I hated—loathed—for at least four years but was afraid to leave. Working every day, always complaining about the job, the lack of pay, my inability to use my skills. I could have been an excellent employee but instead, I was a loafer. My disease of food addiction and fear and doubt had me sitting in self-pity. Oh, poor me. Oh, poor pitiful me. I didn't believe in my ability. At the time, I was going through a separation and divorce. I was paralyzed by my emotions and I saw myself as a victim instead of a victor. Where was my high resolve, my determination, my strength, and my faith? Fear took over day after day. Sometimes I felt on top of the world after speaking to a man—any man would do. He could have been married, in a committed relationship, or on a 1-800 man, it didn't matter. I wanted to feel good, not sad, depressed, lonely, angry, or miserable. A piece of fine China thrown down on a concrete porch—shattered in a million pieces that only God could put back together. Are you open to letting God put your broken pieces back together?

Chapter 11

Woman, who do you believe you are? I recently read a quote that simply stated, 'You are smarter than you think, braver that you believe, and twice as beautiful as you ever imagined." I don't know who wrote it, but it is a quote I would like to remember to say daily. It is likely it will alter the way one think about themselves. I don't know about anyone else, but it is easy for me to find everything that is wrong, but it is better to focus on what is right. I look in the mirror today and I see a beautiful, loving, kind, happy, joyful, funny, and friendly woman. I also see a woman who has risen above her circumstances not because she's smarter than anyone else, but because she has a loving Father who loves and cares for her and He reminds her of who she is.

Your Heavily Father, The Alpha and Omega wants more for you too. Take a moment and stop to look in the mirror—really look! I know it may be difficult for some of you to do this, believe me, I understand. I used to have a difficult time looking at myself in the eyes. It was a challenge for me as well because there was so much pain on the inside, I didn't love the person looking back at me and I was dishonest about so much. Sometimes it's necessary to take a second and third look because at first glance we could not look long without a tear falling down our cheeks or say a negative word.

Be kind to yourself—you deserve it. This may be difficult for those who have been told as a child, teen, or adult that you were nothing and was not going to be or do anything valuable. Maybe someone called you worthless, fat, or ugly. Maybe you were ignored and talked about behind your back. I remember a time when some good old Christian women talked about a young lady in my presence. When the young lady was at work, she was the best thing since sliced bread. I didn't have anything to lose so I stated firmly, if you ever want to talk about me, come say those things in my face not behind my back. I never had to hear them talk about another person. I have to say I still get a good laugh out of that incident. Lady hold up your head! All of the trials and tribulations you have endured have been pruning you for something greater. Go Lydia, Queen Esther, Mary, Martha, unnamed woman with the issue of blood and take your place. You deserve to be placed in high places in the physical realm as you already have a place prepared for you in heavenly places—humbly and graceful.

While I don't have all of the answers on how to fix all of life's problems, I can honestly say that the process of discovering or rediscovering self through Christ is not easy but rewarding. It may even be a slow process, but allow God time to work on you. Think about clay when it first starts out, it's hard, cold, and a ball of nothing. But when the potter takes it into his hands to begin shaping it, he might break some off, then put it on the wheel. After God has in His mind what he wants to do with it, He turns the wheel around and around, puts some water on it to make it more pliable. He then begins to shape it, but sometimes it goes too far to the left or right and he has to either destroy it and begin again, or he can make a slight adjustment to get it like he wants it. The finished product has not been presented; yet, as this process can go on for hours.

Once he has finished shaping it, it still isn't a finished product because it has not been heated up so that the painting can take place. He might also want to add some design on the pottery, which is done prior to the heating. The heating allows it to stay in the shape the potter wanted it so that he can paint it so that it can be used. Then the painting is completed and someone else can now use it for its intended purpose. That's what the potter does with us. God molds us, but sometimes we go off the path that was chartered for us, and we have to be brought back on the right path. This detour takes us through a sometimes-long journey in which may keep us in the wilderness longer than God had intended. He attempts to get our attention, but we are sitting in a corner or lying on the bed with tears flowing down our face, or sitting in a bar with a tall drink to drown our sorrows, or even eating a half gallon of butter pecan ice cream and a bag of cookies to drown our sorrows. Then you go to the doctor because something isn't right. The doctor says you may have had a heart attack, or you have high blood pressure, or you had a mild stroke. Does God get your attention then? God doesn't cause these things to happen, but He will allow the enemy to throw you a curve ball to see if you will remain faithful. Perhaps you will get back on track and get on your knees and ask God for help. While this isn't what the enemy wants, God does. Many characters in the Bible went off and did their own thing because they didn't want to do something hard. Let's take a look at Moses. He didn't want to go to Pharaoh and ask him to let the Israelites go because of his speech impediment. Another character, Jonah, didn't want to go deliver a message to the people of Nineveh, so he sailed away and was eaten by a whale. Eventually he went and did as God had instructed him. God gave the Israelites everything they needed after they were delivered from the Egyptian's rule, but they complained the entire time and were very disobedient. Since they didn't like what God was doing nor how he was doing it, they did their own thing and ended up making a 40-day journey into a 40-year journey. Have you ever felt like you could have done something a whole lot quicker if you had just listened to God or better yet asked God first?

Chapter 12

Before returning home after my extended vacation, I made a few calls to people who said, "If things don't work out there, you can have your job back." Or, "If things don't work out, we have a place in our home for you." Those were lies as well. I went back to the job I hated, and could you believe they didn't have a job for me? I had only been gone nine weeks. They had not even hired another person. Lies all lies. OH, and the friends who said they would have a place in their home, they didn't, but they had plenty of excuses. *What am I going to do?* I thought. So, my beautiful daughter and son-in-law offered their home to me until I could find a job. Let's just say that didn't go very well and I moved on. Consequently, that ex-husband sent word through my son that I could come and sleep on his sofa because he didn't want to see me homeless. Well, I took him up on it because this man owed me. He left me with debt from fixing up the house and not enough money to live on while he was buying her things and taking her on trips and later bought him a home. The home he bought was one that he and I had looked at that we wanted to retire in once the children were gone. What nerve?!

His home was a ranch style patio home with two bedrooms, two bathrooms, and an office which was situated in between the bedrooms. His home was always clean and well decorated. When we were married, he would bring home the drapes and furniture and do the decorating. I rarely had to do anything in that department, which was fine with me. Whenever you finished your meals, he didn't want one dish in the sink since the dishwasher was conveniently situated next to the sink. Very rarely would you even find a glass on the kitchen counter. While he had this beautiful wooden octagonal table in his kitchen, people normally sat on the bar stools at the counter situated between the kitchen and family room. The family room was furnished with beautiful neutral tones and a flat screen television mounted on the wall above the fireplace. Above his kitchen counters sat a couple of ceramic roosters and a few other odds and ends yet tastefully arranged. The bedrooms were decorated nicely, and the home was always clean probably because he was rarely there. I lived in his home for three long months. I'm sure I caused some headaches while I was there, but he was very generous. I didn't have a job, nor did I have any money. The Word says God will make your enemies your footstools. Well, here is the man who left me for another woman providing a place for me to live rent free.

God put on people's hearts to give me money to buy food and gas so that I could get to meetings, church, grocery store, or job hunt. I knew that I didn't want to stay there forever so I looked online everyday but that wasn't enough for him. So, I went to the mall and secured a position. Thank God—a job. It wasn't much, but I was grateful. thereafter I was hired for a full-time job that would allow me to move out of his home. I couldn't get out of there fast enough. I was going to miss my son since he lived there also, but this was necessary. God was still working on me to mold me into the woman he wanted me to be and appreciate. Everything was starting to look up or was it? Life during this time was interesting to say the least. Working in a card store at the mall provided a lot of perspective and gratitude. Perspective in a sense that I really appreciated my journey, and I could have been on the street without a job. Gratitude because I had a place to live, food to eat, clothes on my back, and a job no matter what the pay was. The company I really wanted to work for had yet to call so I became very persistent. How many know if you want something, you have to go after it, it's not going to come to you. I became the annoying fly around the picnic until someone would interview me. That persistence paid off because

I secured an interview and a position with this company—with whom I am still employed.

In order to move to the next level, it was important to budget the finances God had given me. I wish that I could say that I had this down and there was no problem releasing my tithes, but I did have some apprehension because I didn't make much. What I learned in the financial class at church was that God only asks that I tithe to see where my heart was. God doesn't need my money. While I was living with my parents, I was taught to tithe and then pay myself the same ten percent. If I had been obedient, I would not have had any financial problems, but I didn't because I was afraid of not having enough. So, I decided to try tithing with my eyes closed and trust that God would supply all my needs, and believe me, that is exactly what happened. A few months after working two jobs, I received a call from a family member asking if I wanted to rent a room in his home. This move would allow me to get to know a couple of my family members more. This was a new beginning.

This new beginning brought me more peace and harmony in my life. I went from sleeping on the sofa of my former spouse to renting a room. However, my past would soon catch up with me. The moves and money issues that I encountered over the previous months put my car payments behind. The finance company called me several times and I informed them that the car was exactly where I told them it was, but they were unable to locate it. God was protecting me from being stranded and wanted me to turn in the car before it was repossessed. But I was afraid. Afraid of not knowing how it was all going to work out. What I know now more than I did then is God is not going to lay the plans out for us and say, this is what I want you to do and then I am going to do this. Faith was necessary for the plans to work out the way God wanted it to happen, but fear stepped in. There again, the enemy came to divert me away from the promise God had in store for me, but that was not the end.

Yes, the car was eventually repossessed, but something happened that old Satan didn't plan on—I was happy. While walking to the bus stop the morning after they picked up the car, I began to think about what God was going to do to change my situation. Day after day I rode the bus to work or to meetings or to the grocery store. Less than a year later, I moved into my own apartment. This apartment was a mile from my job. I'm still amazed at how God moved in my life during that time. It was all perfect because it was not orchestrated by me. The walks to work provided exercise and allowed me to appreciate nature, the birds sounded even more beautiful than before. The trees looked even greener than before. That little one-bedroom apartment was the best place I had ever rented because it was my first apartment by myself. Prior to moving, I had a vision of what I wanted in an apartment, I knew how much I wanted to spend, and I knew it had to be convenient to work. I got that and a whole lot more. Never let go of your vision, your dream. In Habakkuk, it says to write down your vision and make it clear. Every time I have used that passage and told God to let His will be done, I get just that. My plans don't always happen the way I want them to happen or in the time frame, they rarely do, but they do happen better than I expected.

Chapter 13

God took that broken little girl and made her into a Diamond! God can do the same for you if you let Him. Let go of the heavy rocks weighing you down.

After being tossed aside and beaten down, God lifted me up and gave me a new life! A life I Love. It's not perfect by any stretch of the imagination, but it's more than I could have imagined.

The man that continued to pursue day after day, month after month, year after year recently became my husband. It was not an easy road because we both had issues to deal with, but more importantly, I stopped letting past disappointments, hurts, lies, losses, and fears keep me from moving forward. I heard a song recently that just reminded me that my past is behind me and it's time to see what God really has for me. I cannot move forward always looking in my rearview mirror. Not to mention, I just might run into something in front of me and cause some damage. My view is a lot clearer in front of me. Life won't be perfect, and our marriage may have some situations that we will have to work out as a couple, but I would rather go through life with him than not. When I said that to myself out loud, I knew that I needed to let him know that I was ready to marry him.

How did we get there? He had asked me to marry him a couple of times, but when it didn't happen in my time, I no longer wanted to talk about it. It is necessary for me to mention that he was diagnosed with an illness that could take his life in five years. I had said I often asked people's opinions on what I should do so I expressed my concerns and fears. Most people asked, "Do you want to raise more children? Do you want to be taking care of a man the rest of your life—you're young and active?" I listened to them, but I should have gone to God and asked Him what I should do. Everyone has an opinion, and it may be good for them, but not for you. There are some women who are miserable, and they can't see anything good in their life so they are going to share where they are not where they would like to be. Some people cannot give hope in a dark place—only more hopelessness and feed into your fears. Quite often I found myself comparing myself with others and being stuck. How many know staying still is not possible—you're either going backwards or forwards. I choose forward today.

Let me tell you just how God moves when we follow God's lead. Once we decided when we were going to get married, we decided it was going to be simple. This was during a pandemic and we didn't need to be around a lot of people—just family and close friends. My husband's doctor is over a medical institute and was able to secure the chapel for our ceremony. Okay that's cool. Once he notified us a few days later, a lovely woman contacted me to go over what we needed. I didn't need anything—I hired a photographer, ordered flowers, and asked my daughter to handle some of those details. I bought my dress, all was good. The following events could have only been directed by God. She contacted me the following day to let me know that one of their partners had heard about us and wanted to make our day special. They were going to buy food, flowers, pay for the photographer, and anything else that I needed. Oh, my goodness! Are you kidding? I was speechless. Since we already had a photographer, we decided to keep them. We weren't buying any food. We wanted everyone to come but to go home afterwards. I was so excited I was about to come out of my skin. The day of the wedding was more than I could have ever imagined. The weather was beautiful, people took care of me, and loved on me. I had my makeup done and another friend helped me dress. This is a woman who had so much fear, doubt, and insecurity that she didn't have a lot of friends but God. I asked God many years ago to send me true friends, not people who said they were my friends and then disappeared when they didn't know what to do because life changed. I have also asked God for discernment so that I would know who was worthy to be in my inner circle. The chapel was decorated with flowers and bows—how beautiful. When I arrived, I was greeted by my beautiful children, my pastor, and one of the coordinators to make sure I had everything I needed. When I walked into that chapel, I was greeted by my soon-to-be husband with smiles and surrounded by 12 friends and family as well as several via Zoom. I wish I could express how amazing our day was. If you have ever asked for a special gift but wasn't sure that you were going to get it because the funds looked kind of funny but when you least expect it, you get this gift. Imagine what that was like whether you were an adult or child, the feeling is the same. I am blessed to now have six children and three grandchildren, a host of cousins and aunts that I didn't have before.

I would like to say that I have it all together, but I don't. God is still working on me. There are days when I can still have some doubt and insecurity, but I am reminded when I hear the Word or read the Word that I am more than enough through Jesus Christ. I can't wait to see what else my Heavenly Father has in store for me!

I would like to say that I have it all together, I treat my husband well all the time, and it's great everyday but that would be a lie. There's still some growth that needs to take place because I'm human and God is not finished with me yet. As long as I am still moving and breathing, I still have time.

Keep looking forward and don't stop moving--I didn't and my journey continues.

Made in United States
North Haven, CT
30 September 2022